WHO IN THE WORLD IS IN CHARGE?

★★★

GERALD GARDNER

A PERIGEE BOOK

To Karen and Lindsay Gardner
The Golden Couple

Perigee Books
are published by
The Putnam Publishing Group
200 Madison Avenue, New York, NY 10016

Photographs courtesy of UPI/Bettmann, Wide World Photos,
The White House, and Gerald Gardner.

Library of Congress Cataloging-in-Publication Data

Gardner, Gerald C.
Who in the world is in charge?/Gerald Gardner.
p. cm.
ISBN 0-399-51650-6
1. World politics—1985–1995—Caricatures and cartoons.
2. Statesmen—Caricatures and cartoons. 3. Heads of state—
Caricatures and cartoon. 4. American wit and humor, Pictorial.
I. Title.
D849.5.G39 1990 90-39745 CIP
909.82′8′0207—dc20

Printed in the United States of America
1 2 3 4 5 6 7 8 9 10

This book is printed on acid-free paper.

AN INTRODUCTION
By Mikhail Gorbachev

First I should explain that I'm not *that* Mikhail Gorbachev. I'm in women's sportswear.

But with the similarity in names, there was a mix-up and they asked me to write this introduction.

So I thought what the hell. After all, who ever asks a sportswear manufacturer what he thinks about world leaders? Except the models.

Besides, this past year the world has gone crazy, right? Lithuania, Panama, China, Romania. It's madness! Worse than anything since the cutters strike.

All over the world people cry out for freedom—there are places where the streets are crowded with teeming masses—where men struggle to escape the bonds of misery. I am thinking of Queens.

So here's my feelings about today's world leaders.

First, they're not what they used to be. Look at *America's* leaders. Where are the Lincolns and the Roosevelts? They're all playing football.

We're lucky to have a man like George Bush. What the world needs is *ten* leaders like George Bush. The trouble is we have *twenty*.

When George Bush was head of the CIA, the Devil appeared to him and said: "George Bush, I will make you President of the U.S. but you must forfeit your soul." And Bush said, "So what's the catch?"

Now what about Gorbachev? (Not me,

the other guy.) Will he survive? Will he let go of the Baltic states? Will he marry again? I don't know. All I know is he is ruining Yakov Smirnoff's act.

Then there's Margaret Thatcher. They call her "The Iron Lady." Either this means she is a strong-willed, determined woman, or else she wears aluminum underwear.

Now we come to a *real* leader—Pope John Paul II. Let me tell you a little story. Picture a young boy growing up in Poland. He lives in poverty but he dreams of serving a greater good. Then one day people speak his name with reverence. I guess you know I am talking about Roman Polanski.

Then there are Noriega and Ortega. I'll tell you a secret. I have a suspicion that these two are actually the same guy. Don't laugh. Has anybody ever seen them together?

Next we come to Toshiki Kaifu, the Prime Minister of Japan. A lot of Americans are upset because Japanese companies have bought Columbia Pictures, Rockefeller Center, and the state of Kansas. Big deal. Think how much better it would have been if instead of bombing Pearl Harbor, they had bought it.

Then there's Helmut Kohl, the Chancellor of West Germany. He is now planning to reunify Germany. Some people worry about this. What's to worry? It's going to be a very careful three-step process. First, the foreign ministers will meet; second, the economic leaders will talk; and third, they'll invade Poland.

Well, that's it. The leaders of the world. Some people say that they're a bad bunch, arrogant, corrupted by power, devoted to their selfish ends and willing to plunge the world into depression and war.

Picky, picky, picky.

I see a kinder, gentler nation and 1000 points of light. But I'm taking a lot of medication.

We're out of bread,
we're out of meat,
we're out of shoes.
What could be worse?

We're out of power.

The revolution has taught me three things. Fight bravely, love Poland, and never wear a plaid shirt in a print chair.

People say Israel refuses to talk to the Palestinians. That is not true. Hi, Abdul . . .
Hi, Mr. Shamir.

Comrades, be patient. Ronald McDonald will visit *all* the McDonald's restaurants.

I'm sending you to Latin America, Dan.
Gee, I wish my Latin was better.

Of course, I paved the way for the breakdown of the Soviet Empire.

Two million dollars for one speech?

You'll notice it's not raining on me.

OF
And Morocco has agreed to send a hundred of these to the Persian Gulf.

We live in a world of constant change. Even as I speak to you, my government is being overthrown.
FORDHAM

Contra? Contra? Nope, doesn't ring a bell.

So, if you don't deliver the pizza in an hour, we get it free? I'm in Poland.

The massacre in Tiananmen Square was tragic. But sometimes you gotta kick some ass, right?

I'm Mikhail Gorbachev. I opened the borders of East Germany.

I'm Ronald Reagan. I open at Caesar's Palace on the 12th.

He's doing the flag bit.

Say thank you to President Bush, kids. He's cutting the Capital Gains Tax.
Prepare To Meet Thy God

It's nothing personal, but I really don't need you around anymore.

U.S.NAVY
Well, there it is, Mr. Yamashita. Do you think it's worth the price?

No, under the new policy you actually have to count the votes.

Europe has nothing to fear from a unified Germany, not as long as *I'm* Chancellor of the Fourth Reich.

What's Ron like
as a lover?
SHOW
Rivers

I think I'm in trouble.

Lech, it's fantastic. They've approved an economic aid package of $40 billion for Poland and Hungary to share equally.
How much do we get?

It's a letter from Oliver North. He says, ''Tell the contras the money's in the lecture circuit.''

ZZ-ZZ-ZZ

If Gorbachev stops sending me money, can I sue?

Now how many
Congressmen are in
the 20,000- to 40,000-
dollar price range?

Never mind the occupied territory. I want Park Place and the Boardwalk.

I should have picked a more mature Vice President. Eight-nine-ten . . . Red Light!

Swinging couple seeks older man . . .
Deus prefere os pobres
Torcida de Deus lota o Maracanã
O SEU ANEL AOS POBRES

Andy Rooney said *what?*

These have been difficult years. Labor unrest, no free elections, Communist pressure. And I have to keep painting this mustache.

You’re right. It’s like talking to Dan Quayle.

But I was told I'd be going to heaven.

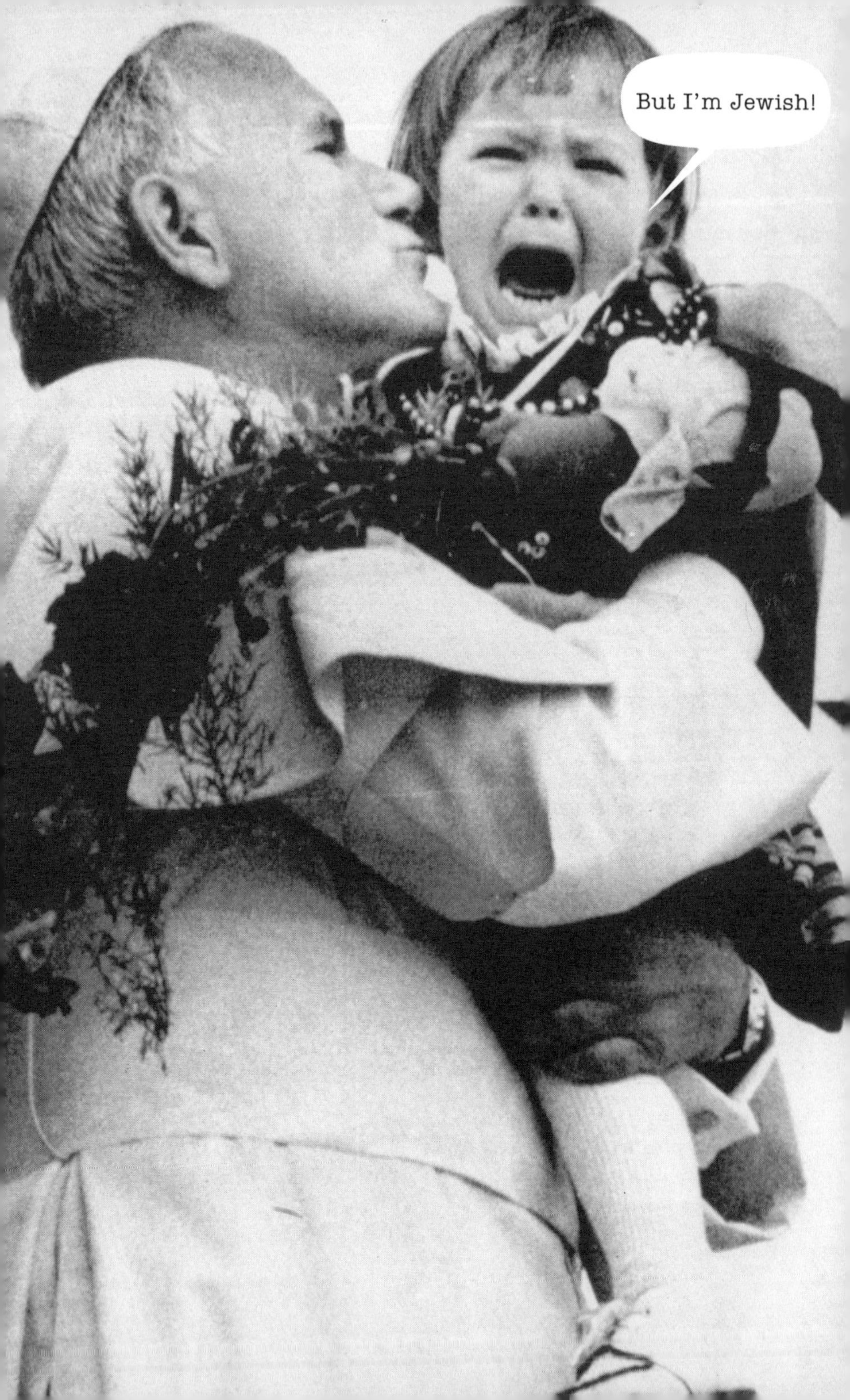
But I'm Jewish!

You're not as popular as you think. Our luggage is in Brazil.

That's how much I left
in the Treasury.

I offered Reagan two million dollars to speak in Libya but he saw right through it.

When you get to Saudi Arabia, be sure to tape everything.

In Britain we have two major parties. The Labour Party, which in America you would call the Socialist Party, and the Conservative Party, which in America you would call the Socialist Party.

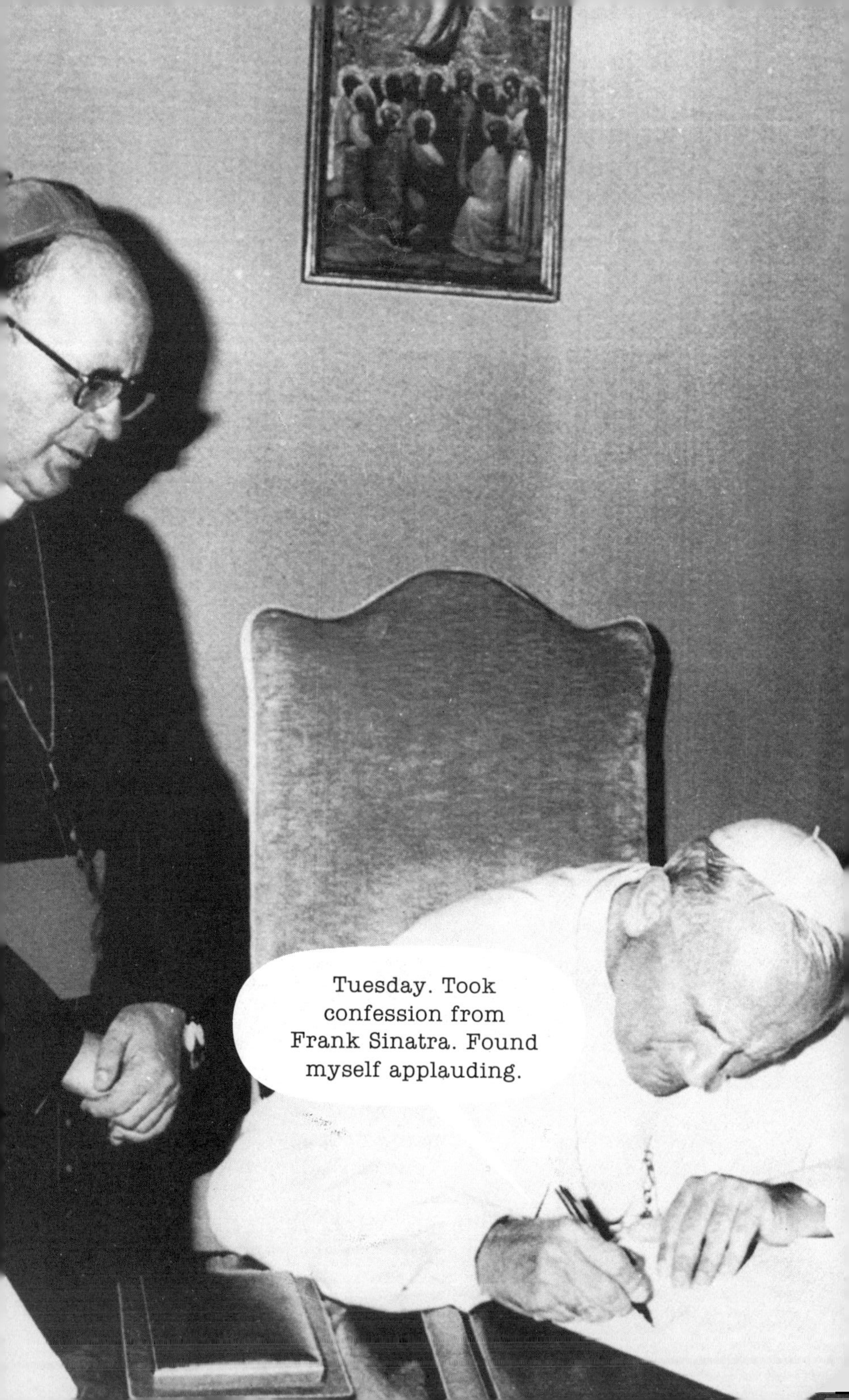
Tuesday. Took confession from Frank Sinatra. Found myself applauding.

First they invade my country, then they throw me in jail, and now they've cut off my CIA salary.

No, no, Your Highness, that's a camel's gonad.

First, you open the package. Second, you unroll the condom . . .

Hm, Mr. Gorbachev has given up on dictatorship. He no longer insists what people must believe or not believe. He's letting people follow their own consciences. We might try that sometime.

Our Father, keep
America strong, keep
the world free, and keep
his cholesterol high.

Well, I wouldn't say that I brought about the downfall of the Soviet Union, but then again, I wouldn't deny it . . .

And this is how we confound the assassins.

It's my new slogan to help the homeless—just say no to poverty.

No, no, no. Toto is the dog in The Wizard of Oz. My name is Tutu.

President Bush has been kind. He helped equip our army. Unfortunately he made all the sleeves too long.

When I open my eyes, there'll be toilet paper for everybody.

I always find a little change behind the cushion.

Lech, I think that money
was for economic aid.

This Jane Fonda workout is murder.

The downside is, if I ever go back to Shakey's, they'll want their tablecloth back.

I'll be frank with you.
Dan Quayle is shallow,
vicious, and stupid.
I like him.

Can we agree to ban nuclear weapons without getting in trouble with the NRA?

Then it's settled. You support Iraq against the U.S., and I don't explode the bomb under your chair.

Sharon and Shamir can battle it out. I'm opening a delicatessen here.

Remember the rules. Only one touch per person.

UNA VIA
They're not having much luck in assembling an impartial Noriega jury.

True, Hussein has a million men, five thousand tanks and poison gas. But we have this.
-ZC

No, it's on the other side.

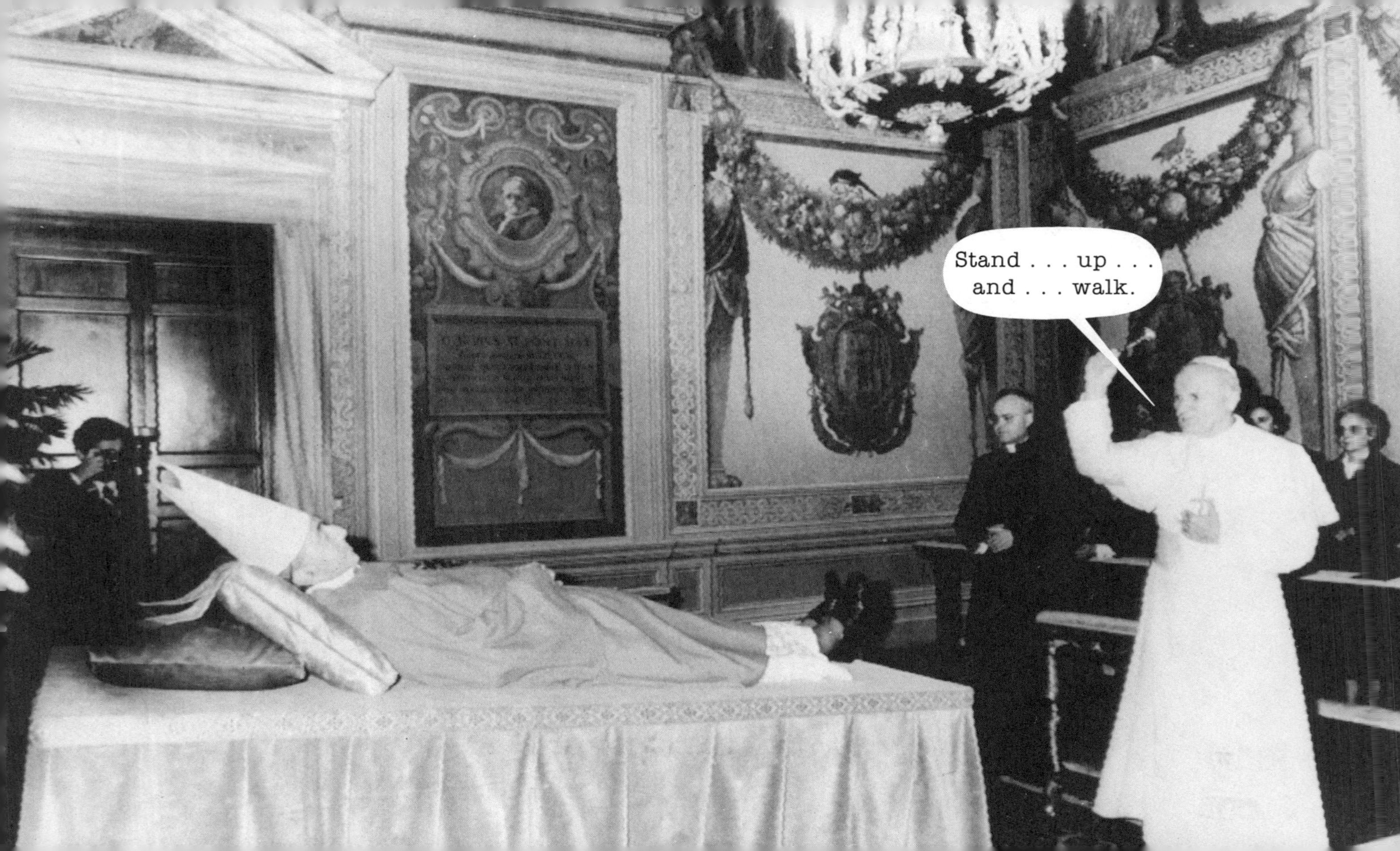
Stand . . . up . . .
and . . . walk.

Leonid, do you have an assistant named Gorbachev who has some strange ideas?

We have problems in Iraq, Japan, Eastern Europe and with the deficit. Which decision do you want to tackle first?
Should I order the meat or the fish?

Remember, not a word about this to Raisa.

I *told* you it was formal.

Great news, comrades. The province of the Ukraine does not want to secede.

So here's the idea. A syndicated game show with you as the host. Barbara turns the wheel and contestants try to read your lips.

I've been overlooking
our ties with Japan.
I haven't been on
Japanese soil since my
last trip to New York.

Okay, I guess that's all right then. There was a rumor you were killing students.

Now President Gorbachev will lead us in a chorus of ''The Party's Over.''

And President Bush, when you visit South Africa you will be free to sit at *our* lunch counters.